SCIENCE QUEST

The Search for

Cures from the Rain Forest

by Carol Ballard

GARETH**STEVENS**
GS
PUBLISHING
A WRC Media Company

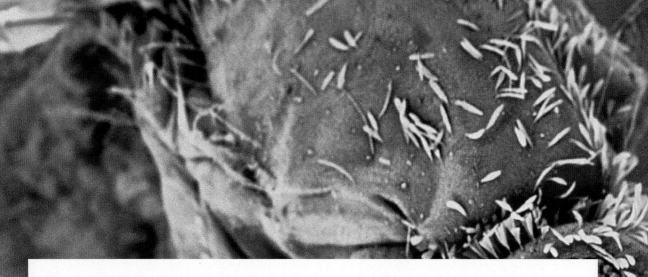

Please visit our web site at: www.garethstevens.com
For a free color catalog describing Gareth Stevens Publishing's list of high-quality books
and multimedia programs, call 1-800-542-2595 (USA) or 1-800-387-3178 (Canada).
Gareth Stevens Publishing's fax: (414) 332-3567.

Library of Congress Cataloging-in-Publication Data

Ballard, Carol.
      The search for cures from the rain forest / Carol Ballard. — North American ed.
          p. cm. — (Science quest)
      Includes index.
      ISBN 0-8368-4554-4 (lib. bdg.)
      1. Pharmacognosy—Juvenile literature.   2. Rain forest plants—Juvenile literature.   3. Medicinal plants—
Juvenile literature.   I. Title.   II. Series.
      RS160.B355   2005
      615'.321—dc22   2004059122

This North American edition first published in 2005 by
Gareth Stevens Publishing
A WRC Media Company
330 West Olive Street, Suite 100
Milwaukee, WI 53212 USA

This U.S. edition copyright © 2005 by Gareth Stevens, Inc. Original edition copyright © 2004 by ticktock Entertainment Ltd.
First published in Great Britain in 2004 by ticktock Media Ltd., Unit 2, Orchard Business Centre, North Farm Road, Tunbridge Wells,
Kent, TN2 3XF, UK.

Gareth Stevens editor: Jim Mezzanotte
Gareth Stevens designer: Kami M. Koenig

Photo Credits: (t=top, b=bottom, c=center, l=left, r=right)
Alamy: 4-5 (c), 5 (t), 7 (r), 9 (t), 14 (c), 18 (cl), 18 (bl), 19 (all), 20 (all). Art Archive: 24 (cb), 26 (tl). Corbis: 10 (bl), 11 (all),
22 (cl), 22-23 (c), 23 (br), 24 (tl), 26 (c). Bodleian Library: 6 (cl). Science Photo Library: 2-3, 5 (r), 5-6 (c), 8 (cl), 8 (bl), 10(c),
12 (b), 13 (all), 14 (b), 15 (r), 16 (c), 17 (all), 24 (c), 25 (r), 27 (c), 28-29 (all).

Printed in the United States of America

1 2 3 4 5 6 7 8 9 09 08 07 06 05

Contents

Introduction   4

Plants That Heal   6

Finding Rain Forest Plants   8

Ethnobotany   10

Analyzing Plants   12

The Search for Chemicals   14

In the Laboratory   16

Testing on Humans   18

Into the Future   20

Case Study:
Medicine from Madagascar   22

Case Study: From Poison to Remedy   24

Case Study: A Magical Oil   26

Case Study: A New Drug   28

Glossary   30

Index   32

Words that appear in the glossary are printed in
boldface type the first time they occur in the text.

When people get sick, they often take **drugs** to treat their illnesses. About a quarter of all drugs used today contain plant chemicals, and about half of these chemicals were originally found in the **habitats** of **rain forests**. Today, scientists continue to investigate rain forest plants in the hope of finding new drugs that may help fight **cancer** and other diseases.

A Rich Resource

All plants contain chemicals that are called **phytochemicals**. Some types of phytochemicals have healing properties that can help people fight diseases. Scientists search for new phytochemicals in plants from all over the world. They also look for useful chemicals in herbs, such as garlic; fruits, such as berries; and vegetables, such as broccoli. Scientists searching for new phytochemicals focus their efforts on rain forests because the forests provide the richest source of plant **species** in the world. So far, scientists have only studied a small fraction of the millions of plant species believed to exist in rain forests.

The World of Plant Research

Today, more than one hundred **pharmaceutical** companies conduct research on rain forest plants to create new drugs for fighting diseases, from simple infections to cancer and **AIDS**. New drugs are usually developed by teams of scientists who work at universities and at drug companies. Many different people are needed to make up a

Finding useful plants in rain forests is a difficult job. While some plants may be potential life savers, other plants may contain deadly poisons.

4

*A Native **shaman** holds medicinal plants gathered from the forest village of Aska Aja, Venezuela.*

A Race Against Time?

The search for new medicinal plants in rain forests is threatened by rain forest destruction, which is occurring at an alarming rate. When a region suffers from **deforestation**, plants that may have been useful are often lost. In addition, people who live in the region may leave. Their knowledge of medicinal plants is then dispersed and eventually forgotten.

research team. **Botanists** conduct the plant research and collect plants from rain forests. **Ethnobotanists** talk to people who live in rain forests to learn valuable information about **medicinal** plants. **Conservationists** may help to make sure that habitats are not damaged by the collecting of plants. **Chemists** find chemicals in plants, and both chemists and **biologists** test the chemicals to learn what effects they may have on living **cells**. **Toxicologists** and **geneticists** check for possible dangers in using the drugs and establish the best amounts to use.

A research scientist takes potentially valuable compounds from plant matter.

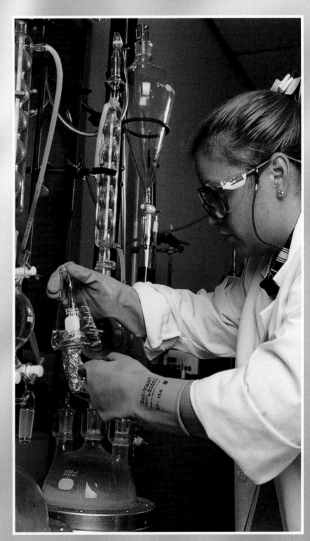

5

People have been using plants to make medicines for thousands of years, in many parts of the world. Some traditional medicines made from plants have no real medical value. Other traditional medicines, however, contain powerful drugs that are the basis for many modern medicines. The scientific search for drugs in plants began in the nineteenth century.

▲ *A page from* Das Buch der Nature, *written in 1475. It is thought to be the oldest published book on plant medicine in the world.*

A Long History

Plants have probably been used as medicine for as long as humans have existed. Written records indicate that Greeks and people from the Middle East used medicinal plants about the fifth century B.C. About 2700 B.C., the Chinese emperor and **herbalist** Shen Nung compiled a book of plant medicine called the *Pen Tsao Kang Mu*. **Archaeologists** working in ancient Egypt have recovered medicinal plants from pyramids. By the first century A.D., knowledge of medicinal plants was considerable. In 78 A.D., a Greek physician named Dioscorides wrote *De Materia Medica*. It listed over six hundred medicinal plants and influenced physicians for hundreds of years. The blending of medical science with botany started in sixteenth-century Switzerland, where a doctor named Paracelsus began exploring ways of using plant chemicals to cure the sick. In eighteenth-century England, a doctor and botanist named William Withering studied the use of plants as medicine. He discovered that an herb called foxglove could treat heart problems.

SCIENCE CONCEPTS

Plants in Chinese Medicine

Chinese medicine has traditionally been very different from medicine practiced in **Western** countries. It treats health in a holistic way, using herbs, diet, massage, relaxation, and exercise to combat sickness. Healing plants are mentioned in Chinese writings dating back to 2700 B.C. Today, the Chinese use thousands of plant substances to cure sickness. **Remedies such as ginseng and Ginkgo biloba are still used today to treat a range of illnesses, from coughs to asthma.**

Today, the leaves of the herb foxglove are made into a powdered drug that keeps millions of heart patients alive.

The Birth of Phytochemistry

In 1803, German **pharmacist** Friedrich Sertürner became the first person to isolate powerful chemicals in plants, called **alkaloids**. With this breakthrough, phytochemistry (the study of plant chemicals) and the search for medicinal plants began. Botany became popular and was taught at famous universities of the time. Treatments for diseases that had long plagued humankind were discovered, including a cure for **malaria** called quinine, made from the bark of the cinchona tree. Aspirin was created from the bark of the willow tree. Once the active ingredients of plants were known, scientists were able to copy the chemicals in the laboratory.

A medicine man from Indonesia gathers rain forest plants he will use for healing.

SCIENCE SNAPSHOT

In a recent report, the World Health Organization (WHO) estimated that 80 percent of populations in developing countries still rely mainly on plant drugs to treat illness. People in these countries use the treatments because they are inexpensive and easily available, and they do not carry the side effects of many **prescription** drugs.

Changing Fortunes

By the 1950s, scientists had discovered a number of important drugs from rain forest plants, and they had also created new drugs by combining existing plant chemicals. By the late 1970s, however, this success had mostly ended. Little money was spent studying plants for potential cures, and several organizations abandoned their plant research programs. Then, in the 1980s, with new, advanced scientific methods, scientists again focused on rain forests. They made many breakthroughs in creating potent new drugs from rain forest plants.

Finding Rain Forest Plants

Botanists and ethnobotanists are experts in finding plants, because they know the kinds of habitats in which various plants live. They can identify plants that have already been studied and named, and they can look at the features of new, undiscovered plants and decide how they should be classified. Botanists also have expert knowledge about the structure and chemistry of plants and how they work.

Tracking Down Plants

Scientists estimate that only 1 percent of the world's three to four million known plant species have been studied for their medicinal properties. Rain forests are good places to search for new medicinal plants, because they have so many different plant species. This incredible variety, however, can make it hard to know where to look. One **sampling** method involves collecting as many different species as possible but avoiding those plants that have already been tested in the laboratory. Researchers mark off a huge area and examine every plant within that area. Using this approach, researchers for the National Cancer Institute took more than 45,000 plant samples, and they discovered important anticancer chemicals. Another technique involves looking for plants with chemicals that make them resistant to specific pests and diseases, because the

These botanists are identifying and cataloguing plant specimens in Guyana, a country in South America.

chemicals could have similar effects in humans. A plant with natural defenses against pests might contain chemicals that will provide humans with a defense against diseases. Researchers also focus their hunt by talking to traditional medicine men.

SCIENCE CONCEPTS

Naming Plants

Carl Linnaeus, an eighteenth-century Swedish botanist, developed a system for naming and classifying plants. He gave each plant two names. The first was its **genus**, and the second was its own specific name. The names were written in **Latin**, so that all scientists who knew this language could understand them. Scientists still use this system today. At left is a sample of a weed called *Triumfetta bartramia*, collected and named by Linnaeus.

Safety First

Whether they know exactly what they are looking for or not, botanists have to be careful when they are hunting for plants. Remote places such as rain forests can be dangerous, so the scientists must follow safety precautions at all times to avoid getting hurt or becoming sick. The **environments** they are exploring are home to many living things, so they must also try to cause as little damage as possible. Some rain forest plants are very rare and must not be collected or damaged.

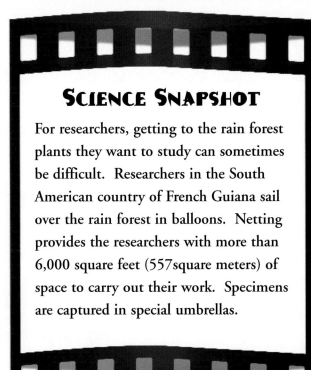

SCIENCE SNAPSHOT

For researchers, getting to the rain forest plants they want to study can sometimes be difficult. Researchers in the South American country of French Guiana sail over the rain forest in balloons. Netting provides the researchers with more than 6,000 square feet (557square meters) of space to carry out their work. Specimens are captured in special umbrellas.

▲
The flowers of the Rafflesia plant have traditionally been used to help mothers recover after childbirth. These flowers are so rare that botanists are not allowed to take many samples from rain forests.

Storing Samples

Many plant-finding teams use portable field laboratories, where they can prepare plants before sending them out of the rain forest. The scientists label plant specimens, so they know where the plants were found and what they looked like in the field. They record size, flower color, and other details that may be lost when a plant is collected. Scientists carefully pack leaves, stems, bark, fruits, or even whole plants. They often pack specimens in special containers that control the temperature and keep plants moist. Some specimens are frozen or dried in special portable ovens. Scientists sometimes carry out preliminary tests on plants in the field laboratory. These tests can tell scientists whether a sample might contain useful chemicals.

Ethnobotany

For many years, scientists did not believe that Native peoples in rain forests had any valuable knowledge about rain forest plants. Today, however, scientists are beginning to realize that a lot of the medicines used by these peoples are actually based on sound science. Many botanists begin their search for medicinal rain forest plants by talking to the people who live in rain forests, as well as studying their written records. This type of botany is called ethnobotany.

Listening to Locals

Ethnobotanists study how people of a particular region and culture make use of the plants around them. These scientists meet with people in an area to narrow the search for medicinal plants in that area. The ethnobotanists give descriptions of particular diseases, along with photographs of the effects of the diseases, to shamans and other local healers. When a shaman or healer recognizes one of the diseases, the ethnobotanist records the plant treatment that is recommended for the condition. If more than one shaman or healer describes a similar treatment for a disease, the plant is collected.

A shaman and his assistant scrape bark from a medicinal plant cut from a rain forest in Peru.

A Head Start

One advantage of speaking to locals is that their knowledge is based upon thousands of years of plant testing on humans. They know which plants are poisonous and can often spot subtle differences between similar-looking plants that might not immediately be obvious to botanists. In the rain forests of Samoa, for example, locals use the bark from a tree called *Homalanthus nutans* to treat hepatitis. Collecting the right kind of bark, however, is not easy for an outsider. There is more than one variety of this tree, and only one variety has the right kind of bark. Locals also know that only trees of a certain

SCIENCE CONCEPTS

Animals and Medicinal Plants

Ethnobotanists can also learn from animals in rain forests. Scientists in Brazil, for example, have noticed that wooly spider monkeys eat fruits of the "monkey ear" plant. Laboratory tests have since shown that this plant promotes fertility. Chimps suffering from infections and upset stomachs have also been seen eating certain sunflower plants. In the laboratory, these plants have been shown to have an effect on stomach pains.

A Matses Indian shaman carries a bundle of medicinal plants gathered from a rain forest near the Javari River, in the Amazon **Basin** in Peru.

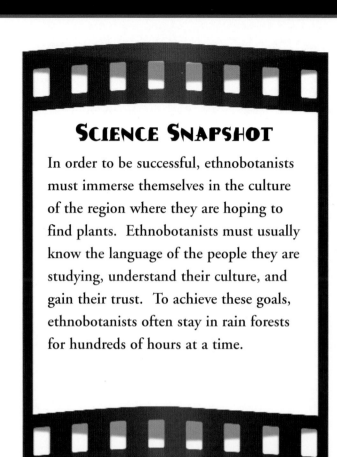

SCIENCE SNAPSHOT

In order to be successful, ethnobotanists must immerse themselves in the culture of the region where they are hoping to find plants. Ethnobotanists must usually know the language of the people they are studying, understand their culture, and gain their trust. To achieve these goals, ethnobotanists often stay in rain forests for hundreds of hours at a time.

size produce a useful **extract**, and harvesting bark from trees that are too small or too big is a waste of time.

Fact or Fiction?

Ethnobotanists must also examine local myths, because there may be scientific truth behind them. An ethnobotanist named Richard Gill, for example, was fascinated by a local legend that mongooses would eat the leaves of a plant called *Rauwolfia serpentia* for courage before fighting a cobra snake. Locals called the plant snakeroot and used it to treat a variety of mental disorders. When scientists analyzed an extract of the plant, they found it was full of **sedative** chemicals, and it made an excellent treatment for high blood pressure.

A Mayoruna Indian tastes the leaves of a medicinal plant while gathering natural remedies.

Analyzing Plants

Once plants collected from a rain forest arrive at a laboratory, scientists try to determine exactly what is inside them. A plant that has been used in traditional Native medicine for a specific purpose may contain one or more useful chemicals that can be extracted in the laboratory.

Extracting and Testing

The first step in analyzing a potentially useful plant specimen is extracting chemicals from the specimen. This extraction can be done by grinding the plant material by hand or by using a special liquidizer. Adding water or another liquid will dissolve some of the chemicals that are in the plant material and get rid of unwanted materials, such as fats. Once the plant chemicals are extracted, they are ready to be tested in the laboratory.

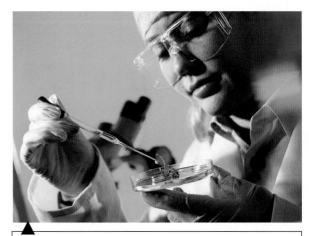

A chemist extracts chemicals from a plant sample using a liquid to dissolve its contents.

Testing Methods

Testing depends on what a research team is hoping to find. If the team wants to develop a new **antibiotic**, for example, they will test a variety of plant extracts on **bacteria** grown in **culture** dishes. A good antibiotic will inhibit or prevent the growth of bacterial colonies but not harm the cell itself.

A poor antibiotic will allow the bacteria to flourish, and the cell may die. A plant extract that does a good job of inhibiting bacteria at this stage will enter the next testing stage, in which chemists will begin to analyze the chemical structure of the extract.

SCIENCE CONCEPTS

Testing With Cells

Animal and human cells can be kept alive in a laboratory. They are stored in special dishes with a liquid that contains all the chemicals they need. The dishes are put into **incubators** to keep the cells at the right temperature. As the cells grow and divide, they are transferred to new dishes. A "cell line" consists of cells grown from one source. Scientists know how each cell line usually develops, so they can monitor the effects of adding the chemical that is being tested.

Different Chemicals

If a plant extract has an effect in screening tests, the next stage is determining what in the extract is the active ingredient. To find out how many different types of chemicals are in the mixture, chemists use a separation technique called thin layer **chromatography** (TLC). Tiny drops of the chemical mixture are put onto glass slides that are coated in a thin layer of **adsorbent**. The chemicals in the mixture are separated because they travel through this material at different speeds, creating a series of bands on the slide. Chemists look at the slide under ultraviolet light to see how many different chemicals are in the mixture. In the next stage of the process, chemists determine the structures of these different chemicals. Each **molecule** of a chemical consists of a specific set of **atoms**, which are arranged in a specific way. When a chemical is subjected to a magnetic field, its molecules give off weak signals, creating a unique "fingerprint" for that chemical. These signals can be detected by a machine called a nuclear magnetic resonance (NMR) spectrometer.

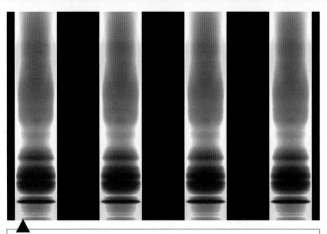

These colored bands represent the separation of different chemicals through the process of chromatography.

SCIENCE SNAPSHOT

INBio, a Costa Rican company, has signed an agreement with Merck Pharmaceuticals, the largest pharmaceutical company in the world, to provide Merck with plant and insect samples for research in return for money and laboratory equipment. If Merck successfully develops a drug from a sample provided by INBio, a portion of the profits will be used to support conservation programs in Costa Rica.

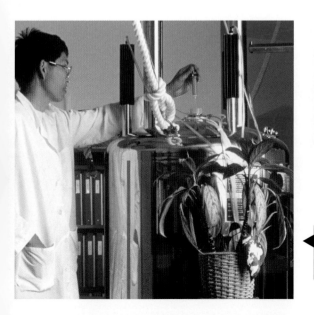

A scientist places a plant extract into a nuclear magnetic resonance spectrometer for analysis.

The Search for Chemicals

After scientists have extracted chemicals from plant material, they have to choose the chemicals that may have medicinal value. All medicines, including those made from plants, can be grouped according to how they affect living **tissues**. The study of medicines and their effects is called **pharmacology**, and scientists who study medicines are called pharmacologists.

Alkaloids

Plants contain chemicals called alkaloids. About 45 percent of **tropical** plants contain alkaloids, which can have powerful effects on other living things. Those alkaloids that have similar structures often have similar effects on living tissues. Alkaloids can be grouped according to their molecular structures. The main groups are pyridines, such as nicotine; tropines, such as cocaine; quinolines, such as quinine; isoquinolines, such as morphine; phenethylamines, such as ephedrine; and indoles, such as tryptamine. Chemists know the molecular structures of many alkaloids. They are not interested in new alkaloids that look similar to the ones they already know, because the chemicals are unlikely to be more successful in treating illnesses than existing drugs. Instead, chemists search for new alkaloids that are very different and may have medicinal value.

Poppy plants contain many alkaloids. Some of these alkaloids are used in medications, including morphine and codeine.

SCIENCE CONCEPTS

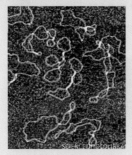

Testing Cells

A human body is made up of millions of cells. Chemicals that act on individual cells or tissues have an effect in a specific area, while chemicals that act on whole organs or body systems will affect the entire body. Before scientists can decide if a plant chemical can be made into a useful drug, they must test what it does to cells and tissues in the laboratory. An extract that works on individual cells to stop them dividing, for example, might be a potential cure for cancer. The micrograph at left shows how an anticancer drug binds to cancerous **DNA**, distorting its shape and killing the diseased cells.

Finding the One

To determine the effectiveness of a new alkaloid, scientists use the same testing process for individual chemicals as they do for the entire plant extract. Each alkaloid from an extract shown to inhibit bacteria, for example, will be tested on culture dishes until the one responsible for inhibiting growth is found. Researchers then know that this chemical has drug potential. By using robots, researchers can drastically reduce the amount of time needed to test plant chemicals. For certain tests, robots can examine thousands of samples in twenty-four hours. In some cases, however, researchers still need years to pinpoint the effective alkaloid in a plant extract. Researchers testing yew extract on cancerous cells, for example, were excited to see that it slowed down a cancer's growth, but the researchers spent years eliminating all the many chemicals in the extract before they identified the effective one.

Copying Chemicals

Once chemists know the structure of a potentially useful chemical, they may try to make it in the laboratory rather than harvest thousands of plant specimens from the rain forest. They might try to modify a similar chemical, or they might try to synthesize the chemical they want completely from scratch. To do so, they mix some simple chemicals that will react together to make new substances. These new chemicals may be further altered by adding other chemicals. Copying plant chemicals, however, does not always work. Scientists are able to copy the cancer-fighting alkaloids found in a plant called the rosy periwinkle, for example, but the chemicals do not work as well as the original plant chemicals.

SCIENCE SNAPSHOT

Developing new drugs is an expensive and often slow process. An average of ten thousand alkaloids must be studied before a promising chemical is discovered. The cost of developing a new drug that will appear on a pharmacist's shelf is estimated to be about $225 million.

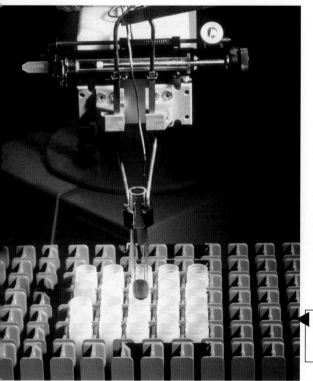

Robots can be used to test thousands of samples in the laboratory.

D rugs must always undergo tests in a laboratory before human trials can begin. These tests are called toxicity tests. Scientists conduct the tests to minimize the chance of any unexpected side effects once people are actually taking the drugs. When doctors prescribe drugs, they need to be sure the drugs are safe and will not harm people in any way.

Toxicologists

Toxicologists specialize in testing drugs to determine exactly how much of a drug should be given and how often. They also test drugs for any side effects and to see if the side effects change according to the size of the dosage. Toxicologists may first test a drug on cell cultures and then later test the drug on animals. They may also test what happens when the drug is combined with other drugs to see if they interact in any way. In some cases, one or both drugs may work better when combined. In other cases, one drug may alter the effect of the other, making it either dangerous or useless.

A scientist examines a cell culture to see what effect a new antibiotic has had on the bacteria within it.

SCIENCE CONCEPTS

Effective Testing

For a scientific test to have any value, it must be conducted accurately. Scientists must consider all the **variables** that could be changed in the test. When testing a drug, for example, scientists could change the amount of drug used, the age or type of cells or animals the drug acts upon, the frequency with which the drug is given, and the combination of other drugs given at the same time. Scientists must choose just one variable that will change and keep all other variables exactly the same throughout the test.

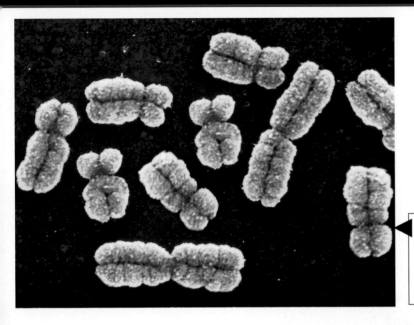

A scanning electron micrograph image of human chromosomes. If a drug alters human chromosomes, it could lead to very serious diseases.

Drugs and DNA

Human cells contain a substance called DNA, which is the genetic material that enables us to grow and function properly. In each cell, DNA is grouped into strands known as **chromosomes**. Geneticists investigate the safety of new drugs by studying the effects the drugs have on these chromosomes. The scientists make sure a drug does not damage or change chromosomes in any way. Changes to chromosomes could lead to cancer. In addition, if a drug affected the chromosomes in the eggs and sperm of people who take the drug, the result might be disease or deformity in children the people might later have.

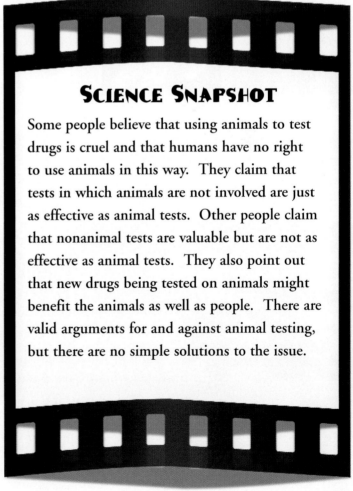

SCIENCE SNAPSHOT

Some people believe that using animals to test drugs is cruel and that humans have no right to use animals in this way. They claim that tests in which animals are not involved are just as effective as animal tests. Other people claim that nonanimal tests are valuable but are not as effective as animal tests. They also point out that new drugs being tested on animals might benefit the animals as well as people. There are valid arguments for and against animal testing, but there are no simple solutions to the issue.

Testing on Humans

Even after toxicity tests have been carried out on a new drug, it needs to be tested on people before it can be used by the general public. Doctors arrange a trial of the drug. In most cases, they must be sure to include both men and women, as well as a full range of ages and **ethnic** groups.

A doctor holds up a new medication being tested as a possible treatment for depression.

Clinical Trials

The testing of a new drug on humans is called a clinical trial, and it usually follows four stages. The first stage involves giving the drug to a small number of healthy people. Doctors observe these people to note any side effects caused by the drug, and to determine what doses can be taken safely. If there are no serious side effects, stage two of the test begins. In this stage, the drug is given to people who have the illness that researchers hope the drug will treat. If the drug has a positive effect, stage three begins, which involves giving the drug to a much larger group of people, sometimes as many as several thousand. This stage can take several years before results can be known. The final stage is conducted after a drug is approved. It takes the form of ongoing studies in large numbers of patients who have been prescribed the drug by their doctors. If any side effects are found, they must be mentioned in the packaging by the drug manufacturer.

SCIENCE CONCEPTS

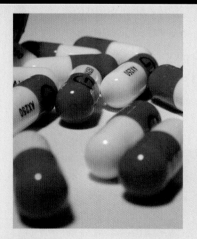

Mind over Matter

Some doctors believe that people who think they are taking medicine, even if it is not genuine, have a more positive state of mind, which might have a healing effect. Since the 1950s, many studies have shown that taking a **placebo** can be almost as effective as taking genuine medicine. The people who have responded best in trials have consistently been the ones who had the greatest belief in the treatment they were taking and the most positive mental outlook.

Conducting a Useful Trial

To ensure that a drug trial is **unbiased**, doctors may give one group of people an existing drug, another group the new drug, and a third group a placebo. The patients will not know what they have taken, so doctors can be sure that differing results will be due to the drugs and not just a different state of mind. Sometimes, an even stricter system called "double blind" is used. With this system, neither doctors, researchers, nor patients know which treatment is being given. The identities of the treatments are not revealed until after all the data has been collected.

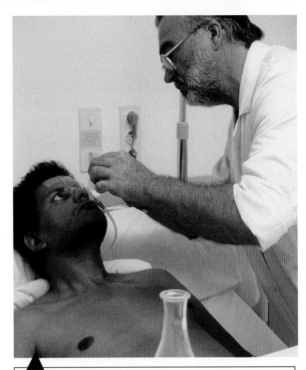

In a clinical drug trial, patients do not know if they are receiving an actual drug or a placebo.

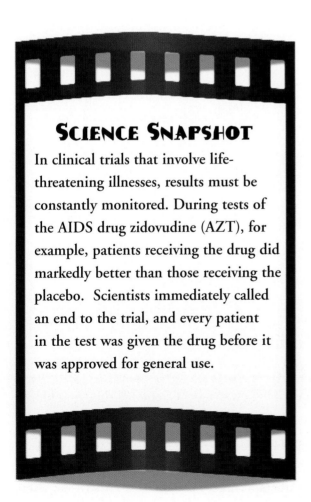

Science Snapshot

In clinical trials that involve life-threatening illnesses, results must be constantly monitored. During tests of the AIDS drug zidovudine (AZT), for example, patients receiving the drug did markedly better than those receiving the placebo. Scientists immediately called an end to the trial, and every patient in the test was given the drug before it was approved for general use.

Measuring Effects

Scientists must decide in advance how they will measure a drug's effect. In some cases, they may be able to take accurate physical measurements. Cholesterol levels in the blood, for example, can be measured accurately by a simple blood test. By conducting this test before and after the new drug is given, doctors can determine if a drug meant to lower cholesterol has been effective. In other cases, however, measurements may involve patients answering detailed questions about how they feel. If a drug is supposed to work as a painkiller, for example, patients may be asked to make a note of their pain levels at regular intervals. These notes will give doctors an indication of how effective the drug is and how long its effects last.

S cientists are constantly searching rain forests for plant chemicals that will cure a wide variety of diseases, including cancer and AIDS. There are millions of plants that may yet yield potentially useful chemicals. If rain forests can be conserved, there is no telling where or when the next important discovery will be made!

Stopping the Destruction

We are in danger of destroying all rain forests and everything that lives in them. Rain forests once covered 15 percent of Earth's surface, but today the amount is 7 percent. Many organizations, however, are trying to put a stop to this destruction. The Rainforest Foundation, for example, has purchased more than 8 million acres (3.2 million hectares) of rain forest and provided it to local people, who have been trained in sensitive farming and harvesting methods that conserve the rain forest. People are also becoming more aware of the need to use lumber that comes from **sustainable** sources.

More than 30 millions acres (12 million ha) of rain forest are destroyed each year. At this rate of destruction, rain forests on Earth will disappear within the next forty years.

Working With Locals

Many drug companies are now working with local communities in rain forests and are trying to record their traditional uses for rain forest plants. These records could be important for future scientific investigations, and **databases** are being set up to make this information available to scientists all over the world. Through programs such as the People and Plants Initiative, which provides support for ethnobotany, conservation, and community development efforts, people can access important information about plants without having to collect and test the plants.

Rain Forest Animals

In addition to plants, scientists are studying other organisms in rain forests for possible new drugs. Chemicals that stop blood from clotting have been found in blood-sucking rain forest insects, such as mosquitos. A new painkilling drug is being developed from the poison of a rain forest tree frog (left). Unlike most painkillers, it makes people alert rather than sleepy.

A Fair Deal

Through the years, large drug companies have taken many plants from rain forests and used them to make drugs. Companies often made huge profits on these drugs, but few of the profits were ever given back to the people in the regions where the plants originated. Today, however, some companies are trying to ensure that local communities in rain forests benefit from drug research and receive some share of the profits made from new drugs. One example of such an effort is the cooperation between the Hoffmann LaRoche company and the country of Costa Rica. The drug company funded a full survey of wildlife in Costa Rica in exchange for plant specimens. It also agreed to share the profits of any drug made from Costa Rican plants with the Costa Rican government.

SCIENCE SNAPSHOT

In many countries, money from tourism is used to protect rain forests. In Peru, for example, the Amazon Center for Environmental Education (ACEER) receives its funding from several travel companies. These companies provide trips into rain forests for people. The companies have pledged to donate a share of their profits to conservation efforts.

By working with locals such as this Cofan Indian from a rain forest in Ecuador, drug companies are learning more about the plants found there and what benefits they might offer.

Case Study: Medicine From Madagascar

Rosy periwinkle is a small, evergreen plant with pale pink and purple flowers. The plant's botanical name is *Catharanthus roseus*, and it is also known as Madagascar periwinkle because it is native to Madagascar, an island off the coast of Africa. Like other types of periwinkle, the plant has traditionally been used to treat many different conditions, including **diabetes**, coughs, and wasp stings.

Despite extensive deforestation, Madagascar still has more than 3,860 square miles (10,000 sq km) of rain forest.

Madagascar Miracle

Western researchers first became interested in Madagascar periwinkle in the 1950's. These scientists were trying to find a treatment for diabetes. They had learned that, during World War II, some U.S. soldiers with diabetes had used Madagascar periwinkle leaves when they could not get any insulin. They also learned that some people in Jamaica used a tea made from the leaves as a diabetes treatment. The researchers Robert Noble, Charles Beer, and Gordon Svoboda studied the Madagascar periwinkle. They found that the plant's leaves contained more than seventy alkaloids. Noble and Beer extracted and purified an alkaloid that they called vinblastine. Svoboda isolated another alkaloid that was called vincristine. "Vin" comes from *vinca*, the old botanical name for periwinkle.

An Unexpected Finding

Scientists found that neither of the chemicals had much effect on blood sugar levels, so they were not going to be effective as treatments for diabetes. The scientists, however, injected an extract of the periwinkle plant into mice that had **leukemia** and discovered that the mice lived longer than they normally would have. The first tests of periwinkle chemicals on humans were carried out in 1960. A forty-nine-year old man who was dying from leukemia was treated with vinblastine, with spectacular results. Within one week, he was able to walk again, and four months later, he was cured. Today, vincristine is the main drug used to treat leukemia in children and vinblastine is used to treat **Hodgkin's disease** in adults. The discovery and development of these two drugs has saved a very large number of lives.

The Power of Periwinkle

Both vincristine and vinblastine work in a similar way. A person with leukemia has white blood cells that are out of control, dividing again and again and making the person very ill. Vincristine and vinblastine inhibit the process of cell division. Although these drugs can now be made in the laboratory, scientists have found that the **synthetic** chemicals are not as effective as the chemicals that are extracted from the periwinkle plants.

Two African girls clutch a sprig of rosy periwinkle, which has been a traditional cure for many diseases.

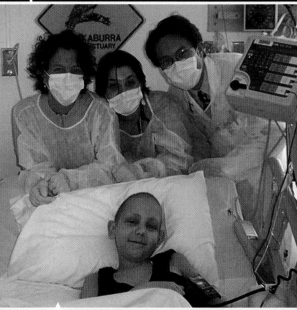

Vincristine can help leukemia victims by preventing white blood cells from multiplying.

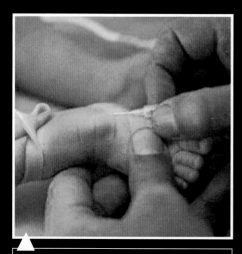

A baby with muscle spasms is given curare.

C urare comes from a climbing vine called *chondrodendron tomentosum*, which is native to the Amazon rain forest in South America. The vine can climb as high as 100 feet (30 m) into the rain forest canopy. Curare was traditionally used by Amazonian Native peoples as a poison, which was spread on the points of arrows and blowdarts. Today, however, scientists have discovered that, used correctly, curare may have many beneficial effects on human health.

Handle With Care!

Although curare can be deadly, it does not act in the same way as other poisons. Curare's active chemical is called turbocurarine. This chemical stops signals in a person's brain from reaching muscles. The muscles relax, and the person becomes paralyzed. When the muscles of the chest and abdomen relax, breathing stops and the person dies of **asphyxiation**. Curare is not absorbed by the digestive system, so meat from animals killed with it can be eaten safely.

Famous for introducing tobacco to Europe, Sir Walter Raleigh also brought back curare from the Americas.

Ready to Relax

Curare has been used in South America as a traditional herbal remedy. The roots are used as a **diuretic** and fever reducer and are also rubbed onto bruises. The crushed leaves are used to treat snake bites. Curare was first reported in Europe in the sixteenth century by Sir Walter Raleigh, a British sailor and explorer. In 1912, a German surgeon named Arthur Lawen first reported that it could be used to relax a patient's muscles during surgery. Two Canadian doctors, Griffith and Johnson, investigated this effect, and their trials, in 1942, showed that curare did indeed relax patients. Curare is now routinely used in certain surgeries in which it is important that muscles remain relaxed, but a patient's breathing has to be supported mechanically. Curare can also be used in the treatment of **tetanus**. Because curare relaxes muscles, it prevents the muscle spasm and paralysis caused by tetanus bacteria.

More Secrets?

In addition to tubocurarine, curare contains a lot of other chemicals. Although these chemicals have not yet been fully investigated, there is a good chance scientists will discover many other medicinal uses for curare. Current research shows that it may help in reducing nausea and vomiting and may also be effective as an anti-anxiety treatment.

The Jagua people of South America still hunt with darts tipped with curare. In Western countries, people are now discovering more positive uses for the plant.

Case Study Fact File

- **Curare was used by Amazonian Native peoples as a poison. Its name comes from two Tupi Indian words meaning "bird" and "to kill."**
- **The poison is deadly if it gets into the bloodstream, but it is safe to eat.**
- **The vine that contains curare produces a fruit. This fruit is also safe for people to eat.**
- **In some countries, curare is used as an anesthetic.**
- **Curare may have additional medicinal uses that have not yet been discovered.**

Chondrodendron tomentosum *is often called velvet leaf because the undersides of its heart-shaped leaves are covered in tiny, soft hairs.*

Case Study: A Magical Oil

The eucalyptus tree, *Eucalyptus globulus*, is a tall, evergreen tree with long, blue-green leaves. It is native to Australia and Tasmania and is the only food that koala bears eat! The leaves contain a fresh-smelling oil that was used as a remedy by Australian **aborigines** for a wide variety of ailments, including fevers, coughs, wounds, and joint pain. The oil that is extracted from the leaves is called eucalyptol.

All-Purpose Oil

A German botanist, Baron Ferdinand von Muller, introduced eucalyptol to the West in the mid-nineteenth century. He thought it would be an excellent disinfectant, and it was used as such for many years. It has also been useful in industry and in making perfumes. Eucalyptol contains chemicals called tannins. When inhaled, these tannins can reduce inflammation of the linings of the nose and airways, which is why eucalyptol is an ingredient in many cough syrups and other remedies for colds. Eucalyptol is also used in creams rubbed onto the skin. As it is absorbed into the skin, it stimulates blood flow, helping to relieve pain in muscles and joints.

The German botanist Baron Ferdinand von Muller

A New Use?

A potential new use for Eucalyptol was uncovered on the outskirts of Sydney, Australia, with a pig called Beau Rowan. This pig had an infected wound on his back leg that would not heal, and his owner thought the pig would have to be killed. As a last resort, a eucalyptus dressing was put on the wound. Within three weeks, the infection had vanished and the wound was completely healed! Scientists at the University of Sydney have since tried using eucalyptus oil, mixed with other plant oils (including lemon, thyme, and cloves), to treat infections in hospital patients for whom other antibiotics have failed. The scientists have found the mixture to be amazingly effective, healing more than two-thirds of the patients. The mixture is still being tested and is not widely available as a treatment yet, but scientists are hopeful that eucalyptus might prove effective against hospital infections.

- Eucalyptus oil was traditionally used by Australian Aborigines to treat a variety of conditions.
- It became known in Western countries in the nineteenth century and was first used as a disinfectant.
- Many remedies for coughs and colds contain eucalyptus oil.
- Current research suggests it may be a very powerful antibiotic.

Eucalyptus is probably best known as the favorite food of the Australian Koala bear.

A eucalyptus dressing healed the wound of a pig named Beau Rowan in Sydney, Australia.

Sprays and ointments containing eucalyptus oil, which can be used to treat minor injuries, are now sold.

Case Study: A New Drug

The Pacific yew is a small, evergreen tree that grows in parts of the United States. Its botanical name is *Taxos brevifola*. This tree grows very slowly, and many of its habitats have been cleared to grow trees for timber. Today, the Pacific yew is important for the cancer-fighting drug that is made from its bark.

A Great Discovery

In 1962, botanists collected a bag of Pacific yew bark and sent it to the laboratories of the National Cancer Institute. When scientists extracted material from the bark and studied it under a microscope, they discovered that the extract was packed with mysterious alkaloids. When tested on cancerous cells, the Pacific yew extract seemed to slow down the growth of the cancer. Excited by this development, scientists injected the extract into mice with leukemia. Again, the extract seemed to have positive results. In 1967, the chemical that was working against the cancer was isolated and given the name Taxol. At the time, however, the National Cancer Institute was investigating several other plant extracts and nothing further was done with Taxol. In the late 1970s, researchers finally began

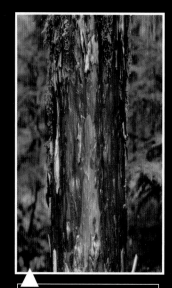

The distinctive reddish bark of the Pacific yew

investigating how Taxol worked. Scientists testing tiny samples of Taxol on various cancers were amazed to discover that Taxol had completely stopped the cancer cells from dividing. In 1982, the first human trials of Taxol began. Taxol could not be dissolved in water, so it was mixed with a substance called cremophore. Unfortunately, this mix proved disastrous, and a couple of patients died as a result of receiving the treatment. In 1985, larger trials began. Taxol's effect on women with ovarian cancer was stunning, and by 1989, it was being tried on other form of cancers, including brain, breast, and lung cancer. Researchers were enthusiastic about the drug, but it presented one big problem. There were not enough Pacific yew trees available for treating everyone who might benefit from Taxol.

A researcher checks Pacific yew plants being dried before the extraction of Taxol.

Successful Synthesis

Conservationists were worried that the Pacific yew might be driven into extinction if it continued to be harvested at its current rate. Chemists, however, had no luck in synthesizing the drug in the laboratory. Finally, in 1993, scientists were successful in making a copy of Taxol. A chemist named Robert Holton found a way to reproduce the chemical from a common form of yew. Drugs companies could now get as much Taxol as they wanted from common yew trees. In the future, it may be possible to make Taxol from a **fungus** that grows on yew bark by growing this fungus in the laboratory. The yew tree is the source of two drugs, Taxol and taxotere, which are currently considered to be the most important drugs used for cancer **chemotherapy**.

Future Treatments

Today, some scientists think that Taxol can be made even more effective if it is taken in combination with other drugs. Researchers in the United States believe that a chemical named beta-lapachone, which is derived from the Lapacho tree in the rain forest, can strengthen the effect of Taxol if it is administered before the drug. Tests on mice eliminated tumors and didn't cause any significant side effects. Clinical trials are planned in the near future, and researchers hope a combination of the drugs will eventually be used to treat stubborn cancers, such as prostate cancer.

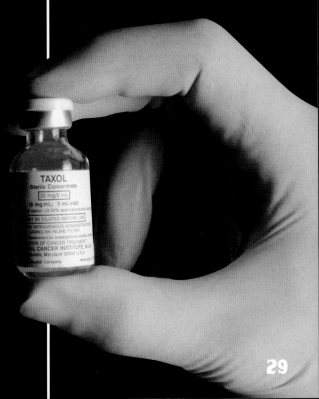

A pharmacist holds a bottle of Taxol, a drug that has proved highly effective against certain types of tumors.

Glossary

aborigines: the first known inhabitants of a region or country.

adsorbent: a material that allows another substance to pass into it.

AIDS: a disease that severely weakens the body's protection against infection and disease.

alkaloids: chemicals, usually found in plants, that have an effect on other living things.

antibiotic: a chemical that destroys or slows the growth of bacteria and other tiny organisms.

archaeologists: scientists who study the remains of past human life.

asphyxiation: a lack of oxygen or an interruption of breathing, causing unconsciousness or death.

atoms: the smallest units of all substances.

bacteria: large group of single-celled, microscopic organisms. Some bacteria are helpful, but other bacteria can cause disease.

basin: the region drained by a river.

biologists: scientists who specialize in the study of life and living organisms

botanists: scientists who study plants.

cancer: a disease in which abnormal cells do not stop growing. Cancer can spread to and destroy healthy organs and tissues.

cells: the smallest units of an organism and the "building blocks" of all living things.

chemists: scientists who study what things are made of and how they change.

chemotherapy: a treatment for cancer that involves using drugs to fight tumors.

chromosomes: strands of genetic material found in each cell of an organism.

chromatography: a process in which a chemical mixture is separated into its components as it flows over a liquid or solid surface.

conservationists: people involved in the protection, preservation, management, and restoration of wildlife and natural resources.

culture: organisms grown in a laboratory.

databases: collections of information that are organized for easy access and are often stored on computers.

deforestation: the clearing of trees in an area.

diabetes: a disease that affects the body's ability to make or use insulin, which controls how the body uses sugar.

diuretic: a substance that increases water loss in the body.

DNA: the chemical in cells that determines the characteristics of organisms.

drugs: chemicals that are used to treat disease or otherwise have an effect on the body.

environments: the areas and conditions in which organisms live.

ethnic: having to do with a group of people from a particular country or culture.

ethnobotanists: botanists who study how people use plants within their local environments.

extract: something, such as a chemical, that is taken out of a natural substance, such as plant material.

fertility: the ability to produce offspring.

fungus: a plantlike organism that must attach to another organism to get food.

geneticists: scientists who specialize in genetics, the study of how traits are passed from parents to offspring.

genus: a grouping of plant or animal species that share some common characteristics.

habitats: the places where certain organisms or groups of organisms live.

herbalist: a person who practices healing with herbs and other plants.

Hodgkin's disease: a certain kind of cancer.

incubators: devices that control temperature, air flow, and light to protect delicate living things.

Latin: a language, originally created by Romans thousands of years ago, that is the basis for English and other modern languages.

leukemia: a cancer of the blood and blood-making tissues, marked by an increase of abnormal white blood cells and a decrease of healthy blood cells.

malaria: a disease carried by mosquitos, common in tropical places, marked by chills and fever.

medicinal: used for treating illness or pain.

molecule: the smallest chemical unit of a particular substance, composed of one or more atoms.

organism: a living thing, such as a plant, animal, or fungus.

pharmaceutical: having to do with the creation or sale of medicines.

pharmacist: a person who specializes in preparing, combining, and dispensing drugs.

pharmacology: the study of drugs, including their properties and effects on living tissues.

phytochemicals: chemicals found in plants.

placebo: an inactive treatment used in drug trials to make comparisons with the drug being tested.

prescription: a doctor's directions for using a medicine, needed for certain medicines.

rain forests: dense forests in warm, damp areas.

remedies: drugs or other treatments used to relieve or cure a disease or illness.

sampling: the act or process of collecting objects, such as plants, for examination and analysis.

sedative: a substance that creates a calming effect.

shaman: in certain cultures, a person who is believed to use magic to heal people, learn the unknown, and control events.

species: a group of organisms that are similar and are able to breed and have offspring.

sustainable: able to be harvested or used in such a way that it is not permanently damaged or its quality is not destroyed.

synthetic: man-made and not of natural origin.

tetanus: a disease caused by infected wounds, the main symptoms of which are muscle stiffness and spasms.

tissues: masses of similar cells that make up a particular part of an organism.

toxicologists: scientists who study poisons and the effects of poisons on living tissues.

tropical: having to do with the region of Earth's surface close to the equator, characterized by a warm, damp climate.

unbiased: not favoring any particular person, issue, or outcome.

variables: in scientific tests, any parts of the test that could change.

Western: having to do with Europe or places settled by Europeans.

Index

AIDS 4, 19, 20
alkaloids 7, 14, 15, 22, 28
animals 10, 16, 17, 20
antibiotics 12, 16, 26, 27

bacteria 12, 15, 25
blood 19, 20
botany 5, 6, 7, 8, 9, 10

cancer 4, 14, 15, 17, 20, 28, 29
cells 5, 12, 14, 16, 23
chemicals 5, 6, 7, 8, 9, 12, 13, 14, 15, 20, 22, 24, 25
Chinese medicine 6
chromosomes 17
curare 24, 25

databases 20
deforestation 5, 22
diabetes 22
diuretics 24
DNA 14, 17
"double blind" testing 19
drug companies see pharmaceutical companies
drug testing 16, 17, 18, 19
drugs 4, 5, 6, 7, 13, 15, 16, 17, 18, 19, 21, 28, 29

environment 9
ethnobotany 4, 5, 8, 10, 11
eucalyptus 26, 27

fevers 24, 26
foxglove 6, 7

genetic material 17
geneticists 5, 17

habitats 4, 5, 8, 20, 28
heart disease 6, 7
Hodgkin's disease 22

infections 10, 26
insects 13, 20

koala bears 26, 27

leukemia 22, 23, 28

malaria 7
medicines 6, 14, 18
molecules 13, 14
muscles 24, 25, 26

National Cancer Institute 8, 28

organs 14

pharmaceutical companies 4, 13, 15, 18, 20, 21, 22, 29
pharmacology 14
phytochemistry 4, 7, 20
placebos 18, 19
plants 4, 5, 6, 7, 8, 9, 10, 12, 13, 14, 20, 21, 22, 24, 25, 28, 29
poisons 4, 10, 24, 29

quinine 7, 14

rain forests 4, 5, 7, 8, 9, 10, 12, 15, 20, 21, 24, 22, 29
rosy periwinkle 15, 22, 23

shamans 5, 10, 11
Shen Nung 6
side effects 7, 16, 18, 29
synthesis 15, 29

Taxol 28, 29
toxicologists 5, 16

vinblastine 22, 23
vinca 22
vincristine 22, 23

World Health Organization (WHO) 7

yew, Pacific 15, 28, 29